# Words for the
# UNBEARABLE
## A Journey Through Loss

ENID SANDERS

JOURNEY PUBLISHING

PLEASANTON, CALIFORNIA

**Words for the Unbearable:**
A Journey Through Loss
Journey Publishing
533 Peters Avenue
Suite 201
Pleasanton, California 94566
Copyright © 2020 by Enid Sanders
All rights reserved

Hardcover ISBN: 978-1-7354348-0-3
eBook ISBN: 978-1-7354348-1-0
Library of Congress Control Number: 2020915177

1. Poetry/Subjects & Themes/Death, Grief, Loss  2. Self-Help/Death, Grief, Bereavement  3. Family and Relationships: Death, Grief, Bereavement

**Cover image:** Bär mit Kind © Michael Sowa

**Printed in the United States of America**
10 9 8 7 6 5 4 3 2 1

# DEDICATION

*To my two Noras,*
*who caught my poems and*
*held them close*

*and my children Karly, Josh, Andrea and Valerie*

*And, of course,*
*in memory of Keri and Drew*

# CONTENTS

# INTRODUCTION

I have had two tragic deaths in my life. When I was 25, my first child died after heart surgery. Her name was Keri, and after she died, I wrote poems I called "Mourning Lullabies" and put them away in a drawer. Almost fifty years later, when my husband died, I reread those poems. I began writing again. Writing has helped me grieve.

The poems are tragic and sorrowful and true. They cover the realities of grief. When the numbness leaves, these are the feelings left to carry.

Besides writing poems, other ways of coping have been useful. In this book, I give them to you in the hope that some may help you too.

As you grieve, allow yourself to just be. Be your own special child and make self-care your first priority. Search out beauty and comfort.

My poems are my journey of grieving. Some may open up feelings and thoughts that help you on your way to remaking your life. I hope they help you see that you are not alone and that you have everything you need to make this journey.

# JOURNEY

Was he your lover?
Was she your friend?
Did you marry?
Did you have a rich history
together?

Did you love him
above all else?

Did she die suddenly
without warning

or

in a prolonged, torturous
manner?

If you want,
take my hand.

Let's sit and begin
the sacrament of grief,

knowing that

it will be hard,
it will hurt,
it will be necessary,

and

it will take some time.

# Mourning Lullabies

## 1971

*"God gave us memory
so that we might have roses in December."*

—J.M. BARRIE

# LAST DAY

Engraved on my mind
your pudgy fist
clutching a string
pulling toy ducks
squealing delight
your last day of life.

# HOSPITAL

The sound of my own sobbing
deafens me.
Nausea engulfs me.
Screaming, wailing stifled
behind closed lips.
The doctor's cold eyes confirm it.
The nurse hands me Raggedy Ann
in a brown paper sack.

# NOT YOU

I search for you
in the faces of children.
Familiar movements, laughter
haunt me.
Not you, not you.
But where, Keri?
I marvel
how far you have wandered
from home.

# TOWERS

Little girl with blocks and bucket
sorting studying building towers,
show me what you've made.
When they topple crumble
crashing, you can't catch them,
I can't stop them.
Don't you be afraid.

# HUSH

Morning
silence.
You are
nowhere.
Somewhere,
do you see the sunrise?
Do you feel
its warmth?
Let its
comfort stop
your crying.
Hush my baby.
Hush.

# GRIEVING

Hidden
in a valley
in my mind,
a sea,
dark and dreary,
without warning,
floods engulfing
all of me.

Pours its waters
through my system,
rushing currents
in my veins,
sudden deluge
evaporates,
painful parching
in my brain.

# SUNDOWN, APRIL 6, 2020

The yahrzeit candle burns

in memory of

a little girl (just over a year old)

and her young mother (just 25)

and the sight of a small white coffin

and the smell of jasmine

and the sound of the Mourner's Kaddish

as they buried her body

(and her mother's heart)

in the ground.

# *Mourning Love Songs*

## 2020

"You will lose someone you can't live without, and your heart
will be badly broken, and the bad news is that you never com-
pletely get over the loss of your beloved. But this is also the good
news. They live forever in your broken heart that doesn't seal
back up. And you come through. It's like having a broken leg
that never heals perfectly—that still hurts when the weather gets
cold, but you learn to dance with the limp."

—ANNE LAMOTT

# Snapshots

―――――――― ⊙ ――――――――

*Be kind and gentle with yourself.*

# SNAPSHOTS

You and me eating curly fries
at Barney's

before

soaking in the hot tubs
in Albany.

The EMTs collecting you off
the floor.

The children standing up for us
at our wedding.

You grabbing the towel rack
as you fell.

Holding hands at the movie.

You hooking up to the dialysis
machine.

The 50-mile bike ride, and

the ER trips by ambulance, and

the 24-hour New Year's trip where
we saw four movies and one play.

Hundreds of pictures
flutter through my head.

## LAST SUPPER

My glass of wine,
you took a sip,
we talked about
I don't remember what.
We touched hands
and sat in the comfort of each other.

# TUNA CAN

Feeling silly, I put a can of tuna
in your shoe.

You said nothing, but
I later found the can in
my underwear drawer.

I said nothing.

The can silently showed up
back and forth for years.

When I think of it,
my heart smiles.

# EPIPHANY

And he said,
"I have an epiphany."
(That's the way he talked.)

And I, drying my hair,
said, "Yes?"

And he said, "I love you!"

I smiled and said, "I know."

And we kept that conversation
in our hearts for 20 years.

And then he was gone.

# GIVE ME YOUR HAND

I can feel the warmth of
your palm,
the strength of
your grip,

your hand so large,
it enfolds
my entire hand,

giving me comfort
and protection.

So

I ask you,
give me your hand,

and I promise,
I will not let it go
this time.

# LAST TIME

When was the last time
we made love?

Was it raining outside or
so hot I opened a window?

I'm sure it was at night,

after a leisurely day and
probably a dinner out.

I so wish I remembered.

I wish I had known then that
it was the last time.

# GIANT BATHTUB

Giant bathtub,
bubbles,
jets,
candles,
music.

Remembered conversation:
When we get old,
we'll need a small trampoline
to get in.

I luxuriate alone in the warmth
like a womb,
like pure closeness,
site of intimacy.

I can almost feel you.

# HOW YOU LOVED ME

I was thinking today about
how you loved me.

How you brought gifts of things you
thought I collected.

How you watched me, pleased,

and brought me

a chocolate muffin that "followed" you home, and
hid all chocolate treats to dole out after dinner, and

I smile remembering

your deer-in-the-headlights look
when I said, "We need to talk,"

which I often said just to see that look.

And I remember

when we first met,

how you touched me cautiously,
carefully, as if I might break.

How ironic because

even when we fought,
you never hurt me.

But when you left,

you broke my heart wide open.

# YOU WERE

You were my sunshine,
the beat of my heart,
the one that I love,
my better half,
my soul mate,
my cheerleader,
my safe harbor,

my person.

# YOUR VOICE

I need to hear your voice.

When I first heard it
(almost 25 years ago)

I was struck by how deep
and strong it was,

a radio announcer's voice—

my own voice so childlike
that callers ask if my mother
is home.

Once you said, in that voice,
"I dare say,"

and I never let you forget it.

I still have your voice on our
answering machine

(impossible to erase).

You say, "This is the home of
Enid and Andrew."

But it isn't.

# WHEN

When I was happy and
you were alive,

I took our life for granted.

Coming home each night to you,

sharing our days,

arguing about the little things,

planning family gatherings,

we were happy and you were well.

But

what did I know?

# YOU IN OUR BED

You cradling me and
me hugging you and
you hugging me and
your hand in mine.

My arm laced in yours and
a kiss on the lips and
your kiss on my forehead and
my head on your chest and

your face in my hands.

# CAN YOU HELP ME?

Can you help me?
I've lost my other,

the one who married me and
lived by my side,

who woke up with me in the morning and
kissed me goodnight,

("Should I cuddle you or
you cuddle me?"),

who knew my victories and
forgave my failings,

who was my safe harbor and
always had my back,

who left in stages
until
he left forever.

# TO BELIEVE

To be held,
to be rocked,
to be loved,
to be safe,
to believe
what is yours now—
mother, brother, husband, child, friend—
will be yours forever.

# TIVOLI

Copenhagen.
Old amusement park.
Haunted hospital ride.
Mechanical doctor waves body parts
and screams at us in Danish.

We laugh until we cry.

Roller coaster.
Dutch woman motions to ask
if you'll ride with her.
Our pictures show her screaming,
clutching your arm for dear life.

You are so approachable
and so safe.

# TRUE STORY

You were here

and

I was loved

and

I tell myself this

because

sometimes I forget.

# Everything Changes

———————— ⊙ ————————

*Reach out and allow yourself to be held by others. Avoid*
*those well-meaning people who don't know what to say*
*or say things that are the opposite of comforting, like*
*"God needed his angel" or "Are you still grieving?"*

# FINAL DECISION

And I said to the children,
"We need to let him go."

And they agreed
because I had the final say
and they trusted me.

And I said (to him)
"Now you'll be free,"

but he was too drugged to answer,
and anyway, there was a breathing
tube down his throat.

And I said (to myself)
"I dearly hope I made
the right decision"

because, after that,
I was on my own.

# I SAW

I saw my husband die
as I sat beside him and
held his hand.

I saw him leave the world
and,
with him,
the life we had
together, and

it filled me with relief because
he was no longer suffering, and

it filled me with sorrow

and

it filled me with the stark truth that this is
how we all end.

# YOUR HAND

Was my hand in yours or
your hand in mine
at the end?

All I know is that
it was a quiet death and
with your last breath, my hand

was trying to hold on.

# I EXPECTED

Some of the changes
came too fast.

Some too slow.

Some dreaded changes
not at all.

Some unexpected changes
hurt like hell.

I was told to get ten
death certificates—

Why?

—and asked (the day you died!)
to donate your corneas.

I was overwhelmed by support
of friends and family,
and disappointed by some.

I expected to get very very sick.
(I did not.)

I expected to be devastated.
(Instead, I was numb and shaking.)

I expected to miss you terribly.
(I had no idea how much.)

I made decisions that were the hardest
in my life,
and still pray they were right.

I knew you would die,

but

there was no way to plan
for the unbearable.

# EVERYTHING CHANGES

Everything changes.

One day you're a child and
the next an old woman.

One day you're a wife and
the next a widow.

One day you're joyful and
the next grief-ridden.

Best to hold on to the highs
when they come

because

everything changes.

# FOREIGNER

Your death
catapulted me
into the foreign
land of widowhood

where I dwell in
loneliness and
memories,

where I sleep in
an empty bed in
your nightshirt,

where I buy birthday
and anniversary gifts
for myself.

# HARD TRUTH

Grief takes its time,

visiting every cell in the body,
every synapse in the brain.

Not attending to
what you want or need,

Grief delivers the message:
"This is real," and
"This is final,"

and,

with a last blow to the heart,
Grief says,

"Deal."

# WHAT'S MISSING

Alone in my home,
among my ideas,
opinions and feelings,

surrounded by all that is mine,

every room inhabited by me,

I miss the surprise that is you.

# WHO AM I NOW?

Alone.
Lonely.
Lost.
Heartsick.
Struggling.
Exhausted.

Widow.

# THE SMILE

As you lay dying,
released from
life support machines,

breathing your last
forty minutes
on earth,

we all strove to
hold, comfort
and support you

in the best way we knew how.

We assured you that you were loved,
that you would soon be free of pain,
that we would stay to birth you through

this final transition.

It was horrible and beautiful,

and,

with your very last breath,

you graced us with a smile.

# I WANT TO TELL YOU

As you slip away in my memory,
I want to grab on,

to pull you back up
so that I can see you clearly

and talk to you directly,

to let you know
I loved you and knew that
you loved me.

Did I tell you enough?
Because
nothing else matters.

# Always with Me

———————— ⊙ ————————

*Allow yourself to just "be" when memories surface;*
*no need to "do" anything.*

# VAPOR

In the night,
in the quiet,

I beckon and
you come to me

in a memory,
a facsimile,

in a vapor
I breathe into me

that escapes
when I exhale.

# BIRD

I suspect that bird is you.

He is in constant flight
from tree to tree
(free as a bird?).

He is the definition of
unencumbered, joyful,
no care in the world,

except when he perches
on the arm of my chair
and watches me closely
with concern.

# FEELING YOU

I crawl into your arms,
feel the beating of your heart,
hear the rhythm of your breath,
hold your soul between my hands,
sigh with relief that you are safe.

# DO YOU MISS ME?

What if you exist
in an alternate world
and
you have consciousness
where
you miss me like
I miss you?

I understand that
I could never
bridge that gap—
countless have tried—

but,

if it were so
that you missed me too,
it would sadden me

because

you would be
in so much pain.

# FLIGHT

When I flew to Seattle,
I had a phantom Drew
beside me and

I watched him read
the three magazines
he brought and

eat his pretzels and
mine too and,

on takeoff and landing,
as usual, I held his hand

because

I am always afraid when I fly.

# ESSENCE

When the house is quiet
and my soul is still,
I can feel your essence
in the hollow of my being.

It says,
"I am here,
you can breathe me in,
you can sense my warmth,
you can be at peace.
You can hold my heart
in the palm of your hand."

# Ambushed

———⊙———

*"Grief bursts" are always powerful, but come less and less frequently as time goes by. You may find that dreaded experiences like anniversaries are not as difficult as you expected. Conversely, small events or memories may be unexpectedly difficult and trigger a strong reaction.*

# ON BART

The tall older man
entering the
BART car

with his bike helmet
and folding bike
is not you.

I weep.

# AT THE READY

I find I clench my fists and
startle easily.

I guess
four years of circling
my ailing husband

in fear that he would die,

and then he did,

has made me vigilant, hyper-
aware that

anything might happen.

# PASSING AMBULANCE

Quiet evening,
pleasant drive.
Sudden
blaring sirens,
flashing lights,
tires squealing,
racing to ER.

I fall apart.

# AT A MOMENT'S NOTICE

Tears live in my head
resting at the ready
right behind my eyes
to stream down my face
at a moment's notice—

when

I hear a sad song,
see your face in a picture,
find a piece of you in a drawer,
hear your voice on the answering machine,
close my eyes to dream.

# THE BULLY

Without warning
Grief tackles me from behind,

full body slam,
no mercy.

Pain beyond measure,
I cannot breathe.

He sits on my chest
and will not get off.

Then,

without warning, he leaves and
I am left with a head full of tears and

the knowledge that
he will be back.

# GRENADE

I hold grief close to my chest
like a grenade
that can detonate at any time.

I think I'll run with it
to another town and leave
before it explodes.

# SURVIVAL

I am often asked how I survived
the death of my baby

and now,

my husband.

I always answer, "What were my options?"

But in truth,

I have "grief bursts" of nonstop crying

and

sometimes go to a place so dark

I think I might die myself.

Then I wonder

if I've survived at all.

# CYCLE

When my vein was pierced,
I bled uncontrollably,
so much that I feared I would
bleed out on my therapist's couch.

Then the blood coagulated
(as blood will do)
and
I carried on with life

until

another blow to my body—
a hospitalized friend or
a traumatic memory—
reopened the blood gates,

and then

I found that the vein
was attached to a
large artery

that went directly
to my heart where
love is stored,

and,

each time I was hit
(suddenly, unexpectedly)

the massive blood rush
would threaten to
break my heart in two.

# CATASTROPHE

---

The wind pulled my neighbor's tree
out from its roots without reason or
ceremony and dropped it randomly on
the front lawn—

the shock of sudden death.

# THE TRUTH OF THE MATTER

Although
I loved them both with
all my heart, and

held him close, and
cradled her near, and

did everything I
was told to do

(and more),

I could not save them.

And so,

I hold my breath around
those I love.

# Letting Go

—⊙—

*There is no correct way to grieve. Grief has its own schedule—it is common to be numb at first.*

# EMPTY

The numbness has dissipated.
The closet is empty.
The boxes and boxes reside at the dump.
The bed is half empty and cold.
Piece by piece and
bit by bit,
you disappear.

# MEASUREMENTS

When your loved one dies,
you know precisely
how much you loved

by

the extent and
depth of your grief.

You know precisely
how much you were
loved

by

the bottomless pain of your
aloneness.

And

you understand your
complete powerlessness

by

your failure
to save them

or

bring them back home.

# CLOCK

Daylight Savings.
Time to change the clocks.

I climb the couch
to reach the one we bought
in Ashland on vacation,

the clock you set twice a year
for twenty years,

the clock you could easily reach,

the clock I look at every day.

I promptly drop it
and
the glass shatters
into a million pieces,

its frame in half.

Nothing to do but
let it go.

# GRIEVE LESS

If I no longer grieve,
are you completely gone?

If I am no longer driven to write,
is there no longer anything
to say?

Will you still hold a place in my heart
and a corner of
my brain?

How will I know you
actually existed?

# I STEP INTO A DREAM

I step into a dream at night and
you are almost always in it.

You are never well and
I am always afraid

because

I anticipate the end
(no spoiler here).

Last night you and my parents
were planning a funeral.

All of you were leaving and
taking Keri with you.

And,

when the sun woke me
in the morning,

I stepped out of the dream and
you were gone.

# NOW IT BEGINS

The painters came this morning
and our bedroom furniture went
out the front door.

(I emptied your nightstand.)

Next week there will be
new carpet in the whole
house.

(I threw out your slippers that
were hidden under the bed.)

Soon your office will be
a sanctuary for our
eight grandkids.

I am making
our home
all mine and

I'm not sure
I can
stop crying and

I can't breathe.

# SOON

On Wednesday,
after your first
birthday away from me and
the world,

I will move your coat and
cap to the hall closet
(if I can) and

I will likely cry and
write a poem because

it is the coat and cap that
kept you warm when
your body was so fragile, and

it was a comfort to see you
warm and safe
sitting in your chair.

## SUPER GRIEVER

I believe that I am a
skillful griever.

I know how to access
my grief.

I know how to
self-care.

I have learned how to
expect grief's unpredictability.

I have reached out and
asked for support.

I don't linger with denial, regret,
or guilt.

I have nailed how to grieve.

I just can't figure out how
to get you back.

# Treading Water

———————— ⊙ ————————

*Sleep when you can and don't forget to eat. Take care and keep yourself strong; you'll have decisions to make.*

# WAIT, WHAT?

I feel better than
I look,

and am worse than
I feel.

I eat too much, and
forget to eat.

I sleep too much, and
have insomnia, and

when I sleep deeply,
I have horrible dreams.

I need to be alone, but
want to go out.

I remember too much, and
forget most everything.

I cry a lot, but
am often numb.

When you ask how
I'm doing,

the honest answer is:

I haven't a clue.

# THE ACQUAINTANCE

You say I am handling death
well and you "don't know
how I do it."

You think you
"couldn't possibly."

You say, "I wouldn't know
what to do without Frank."

Do you think I have options?
Do you think you will?

# THE EMPTY

Feel the empty.
It resides under the heart,
inside the ribs.

With time, it spreads to
the entire body

like a cancer,

encasing the body with
its terrible truth,

that he is gone
and nothing can fill
this void.

# SOME NIGHTS

10:00 p.m.:
Asleep in the tub.

10:30 p.m.:
Bedroom,
tossing, turning.

11:30 p.m.:
Guest room,
can't settle,
itching back, nose.

1:00 a.m:
Bedroom,
restless,
leg cramp.

2:30 a.m.:
Guest room,
wide awake.

4:00 a.m.:
Bedroom,
still awake,
tossing, turning.

5:30 a.m.:
Asleep,
frantic dreams.

7:00 a.m.:
Up for the day.

# THE MAIN ATTRACTION

Here comes the heavy-duty grief.

The other was only the preamble,
the introduction, the preface, the
coming attractions.

Now is the truth of it all.

# SINCE YOU LEFT

Since you left
in a hurry
to escape the pain and destruction,

my heart floats in limbo
looking for a place to land.

# GONE

Everyone out the door
and gone.

Left behind:
the green marker on the kitchen table
misplaced toys
forgotten gifts
someone's shoe
my heart.

# NIGHT

----

When night falls,
reality creeps in,

the world is not safe,

you are gone,

I am alone,

and

the day can't come
fast enough.

# THE THINGS I KEEP

Your grey hoodie, black cap, and
the red blanket that kept you warm.

Pictures.

The hundreds of science fiction and
political books,

although I'll never read them.

The euphonium, recorders, piano and
boxes of music,

although I don't play.

The jars of exotic foods and
strange spices,

although I don't cook.

My love for you and
your love for me,

although you are gone.

# QUIET GRIEF

It's a quiet grief.
It doesn't wail or
howl or keen.

It perches somewhere
in my chest, likely
near my heart,

squatting there, making it
hard to breathe.

# Riding the Waves

---⊙---

*No need to judge whether you are doing grief "right"
because there is no right.*

# THE WAVE

I ride the wave of grief,

which is so high
it blocks the sun,

and, whereas,

in the past months,
I have successfully
clung to
my little raft of containment,

I fear there has been a
shift in the tide

because

when the wave overtakes me now,

unexpectedly and
out of my control,

grief suddenly leaks out
of my every pore and

there is no stopping it.

# LATE RESPONDER

I am not a first responder.

When you died,
I did not truly realize
that it was so.

I lived in my numbness,
doing everyday things
in my everyday way.

Friends said I was
weathering your death
well.

I tried to run from depression.

But now, most every day,
over and over,

I can feel
the swift kick
in my gut.

# ALL IN

To properly grieve,
you must be all in.

No excuses.
No diversions.
No defenses.

Open your window of
tolerance wide

and

be prepared to
burn to the ground.

# FIRST YOU DROWN

I believe that
I need to drop into
the depths of my sorrow
and soak
again and again before

I can even consider
rising up.

# LET IT GO

---

When I can siphon off some of this grief,
I can sleep.

When I can turn off the faucet it pours from,
I can think.

When I can let it drain from the depths
of my heart and soul,

I can breathe.

# WHERE DOES IT HURT?

Your death
broke my heart
shattered my brain
took my breath away
made me weak in the knees
punched me in the stomach
stabbed me in the back
filled my skull with tears
parched my throat
kicked me in the ass, and
burned me to the ground—

but only

when the numbness wore off.

# HOW TO AVOID GRIEF

Left to my own devices I
workcleanexerciseshopreadtalkwrite—

any and all
escapes from the day.

But,

when grief sneaks up,
nothing works

except to cradle it and weep.

# I AM SICK WITH GRIEF

Grief germs lay dormant
in my gut and

crawl up into my throat
whenever the world becomes
quiet, and

then

I break out in tears, sadness,
loneliness and self-pity

that leave

a constant, low-grade
grief fever behind

until

the next outbreak.

# SLEEP AND HEALING

I can't sleep.

I toss and turn and
am awake at
all hours.

I take turns in beds, chairs,
and couches, and,

even though

I tell myself that
no one ever died
from lack of sleep,

I'll bet I haven't had
a full night's sleep
in more than seven months.

Exhausted has become
my resting state,
my default, and

I know that sleep is
necessary to heal
physical ailments but,

what of a broken heart?

# READER

Let me show you,
let me tell you.
Read my poem carefully,

because, if I am clear,
truthful and accurate,

you will be there with me,

if not in time,
then in memory,

and

I can give you a piece
of the nightmare

for you to hold.

# HOW DOES ONE HEAL?

First you write a poem.
Then you read it over and over until
you understand what it means, and

then you send it out
with the hope that
it will be held closely and understood, and

repeat
again and again, and

after days, weeks, months, years,
and countless poems,
perhaps you'll
really know that
he is dead.

# LIFE INSIDE A POEM

Inside a poem,
it is dark and lonely,
but safe.

You don't need to travel
or even
go to the store—

you can go days
without
talking to anyone.

There is ample time
to sit with your sorrow
and grief,

because

life inside a poem
is dark and lonely,
but safe.

# I CRY

I cry

because
my home is empty,

because
the silence is so loud,

because
you suffered and you died,

because
life is short, fragile, and precious

and,

though nature, music, poetry
and those I love ground me,

I cry

because

I am aging and
I, too, will die

and,

leave it all behind.

# RESPITE

When I'm not writing poems,
I'm not thinking of poems.

When I'm not grieving,
I'm not thinking about death.

It seems the mind
and the body
are imbued with wisdom.

That is,

to consider death all day
and night
would be torturous,

as senseless as to deny death.

There is wisdom in allowing
the mind and body
to rest.

# OBSESSION

Soaking in a hot tub,
poetry writing itself in
my brain.

The topic?

Grief.
It's been my obsession
for the past year.

Now

I strive to reenter life,
be in the moment,
take in the days.

Heal.

My patience with myself
is running out.

# Look to the Helpers

———————— ⊙ ————————

*If you feel your grief is overwhelming friends and family,
or you simply want more support, seek out a grief
therapist and/or a grief group.*

# ALIVE

---

In the arms and hearts
of those who see
and hear me,

I am certain I am not alone.

In the arms and hearts
of those who love me
(there are many)

I am rocked back to life.

# ON MEETING ANOTHER WIDOW

Tell me.

Did you lose sleep?
Did you lose your mind?

Did you cry all the time?
Did you almost never cry?

Can you remember his voice?
Can you recall his face?

What do you yearn for most?
What awful memories still live on?

Do you ever not hurt?

How did you survive?

# GRANDCHILD

Livi and I are pruning roses and
smelling rosemary.

Livi says she bets that Papa
can smell the rosemary in heaven

and that

he can see any movie he wants and
not even pay for it.

But, she adds, she'd rather be
watching movies with him.

# LOVED OTHERS

After the dying,
all that is left are the memories and
the others.

The memories and the others
are intertwined
because
the others share the memories.

My others also hold, listen, and
sometimes say just the right thing.

The others can't stop the pain, but
they can keep you from free-fall.

# CONFLICT

I cannot unravel how
my grieving impacts
my children.

How is it for adult children
to see their mother in
extreme pain?

Isn't a mother,
by definition,
meant to be strong

and always caretaking?

Does it overwhelm, confuse,
frighten and confirm that
they are the adults now?

# I Will Survive

———⊙———

*Tragedy often releases creative right brain juices.*
*Journaling, art, and crafting may help you*
*navigate your feelings.*

# MY POEMS

My poems
form a single line and
march over hill and dale through
the road that is my mind.

They hold hands and
sometimes skip and
sometimes sing "I Will Survive."
(At such times I feel foolish.)

Mostly they cry.
(At such times I feel sad.)

All in all, for some reason,
when I let them loose,
they help me heal.

# CALLA LILIES

No matter the poison
from a fumigation,

no matter a deadly germ
running wild out of doors,

the calla lilies push out
of the earth in great numbers,

a delicate and regal white and yellow,

each held up by a study green stalk.

# EIGHT MONTHS

There are whole hours now
when I forget to grieve.

Before it was only minutes.

Sometime, maybe, it will be days.

But

I will always remember that

once

I was just holding on.

# TOUCHSTONE

I am writing a little poem
that fits snug in my pocket
so that

I can reach it any time
like a touchstone and

see a bike ride in Amsterdam or
an anniversary dinner in Paris or

thousands of other memories of
you and me
when you were well.

# WHAT TO DO WHEN YOU LOSE
## A LOVED ONE

---

Be kind to yourself.

Sleep or don't.

Eat or don't.

Stay in or
go out.

Work or
stay home.

Meet with friends or
don't.

Cry
or don't.

Hope that "this too shall pass"
is true.

# RECIPE FOR A SWEET GRIEF

Gather all ingredients,
fresh and true, in a
giant bowl.

Fold in any and all
memories.

Stir very slowly,
adding more memories
as they come.

Sprinkle with
a thousand tears.

Bake at a slow, low
temperature for
as long as it takes

(maybe months,
maybe years)

while you wait, read, write,
rest,
engage some in life

(with care),

and,

when you know you are done,

ingest and savor.

# A PLACE WE ALL MUST VISIT

My plan is to put
aside my grieving.

To let it out the
back door

where it will exist in the
cold and dark

where suffering dwells

until, perhaps,
at some future time

it knocks to come
back in

(rather, forces its way in).

And meanwhile,

I will gather up
all my resources

of friends, family,
home, work,

joy,

and learn to keep
living a full and
meaningful life

so

when grief appears again
(because it will)
in the form of a loved one passing,

I will have patience for a process
that takes as long as it takes,

knowing

I have been there before.

# HOW I KNOW I AM HEALING

The constant tears behind my eyes are dissipating.

The horrible memories are less frequent.

Grief is not a constant companion.

I am less lonely and more involved in life.

I have plans for the future.

I am listening to music.

I am laughing.

I am focused.

I am finally sleeping in our bed.

# FEAR

The secret of slaying the beast,
if you're ready, is to
sit atop him
(best to be surrounded by friends) and—

taking a nonchalant attitude, while
checking out your surroundings
(never expecting a catastrophe)—

repeat the phrase
"I. Got. This."
while truly believing
you do.

# MAKING PEACE

The question, always, is
how to make peace.

Peace when my child died.
Peace when my husband died.

Peace in a world that can be
hateful and dangerous.

Peace in the form of loving kindness,
patience, tolerance, and acceptance.

Peace in the knowledge of my own demise.

# MY MEASURE OF LOVE

Have I said it all?

Because

I have said quite a lot.

In the months since your death,
I have written nonstop about my loss.

I think the equation is:
the more you love, the more you lose,
the less you love, the less you lose.

If I had loved you less, there would
have been so much less to say.

But, oh,

think of all I would have missed.

# CHOICE

I know how to nurture grief.
Now I want to nourish happiness.

I want to be fully aware of
the comfort and beauty
that surrounds me.

To take in the good in the
expanding times when
I let go of the unbearable.

I believe I have the choice.

# IN THE GARDEN

Slight breeze
corner shade
birds chattering
flowers full bloom
cup of coffee
fascinating book
music wafting from the kitchen
no plan except, possibly, nap.

Time to get lost in thought and write.
No intrusive thoughts,
grief tucked away somewhere,
life of ease,
safe, for now.

# DID YOU KNOW?

Did you know that
you will survive the
death of a loved one?

It will hurt like hell,

more than any physical or
emotional pain you have
ever experienced before.

Much more.

And

you will feel angry, helpless,
lost and so many other
over-the-top feelings,

until

you think you might
break—

but
you won't.

However, you will,

if you haven't already,
live this pain some day.

Since

loss is about living,

loss is the cost
of loving and being loved.

# GARDENING

I plan to
gather my poems and

care for them as if
they were flowers
in a garden.

Prune some,
water some,
weed some.

Because

each poem bloomed
at a different time of my
grief,

so that, in tending them,
I can consider
where I was then,
where I am now,
and where I am going.

# YOUR SOUL IN MY HEART

Sometimes I feel you moving
in my heart.

You are settling in for
a long nap,

a nap of sweet dreams and
good memories, and

I know you are there
because in my heart
is where you belong.

# ACKNOWLEDGMENTS

Warm appreciation to my readers Joan and Ray, my editor Penelope Kramer, and my book designer Wendy Dunning.